THIS BOOK BELONGS TO:

THE BACK OF EACH PAGE IS INTENTIONALLY LEFT BLANK TO PREVENT INK FROM BLEEDING THROUGH, WHILE ALSO PROVIDING SPACE FOR FUN FACTS TO ENHANCE YOUR EXPERIENCE AND DEEPEN YOUR KNOWLEDGE ABOUT AXOLOTLS.

COLOR TEST PAGES

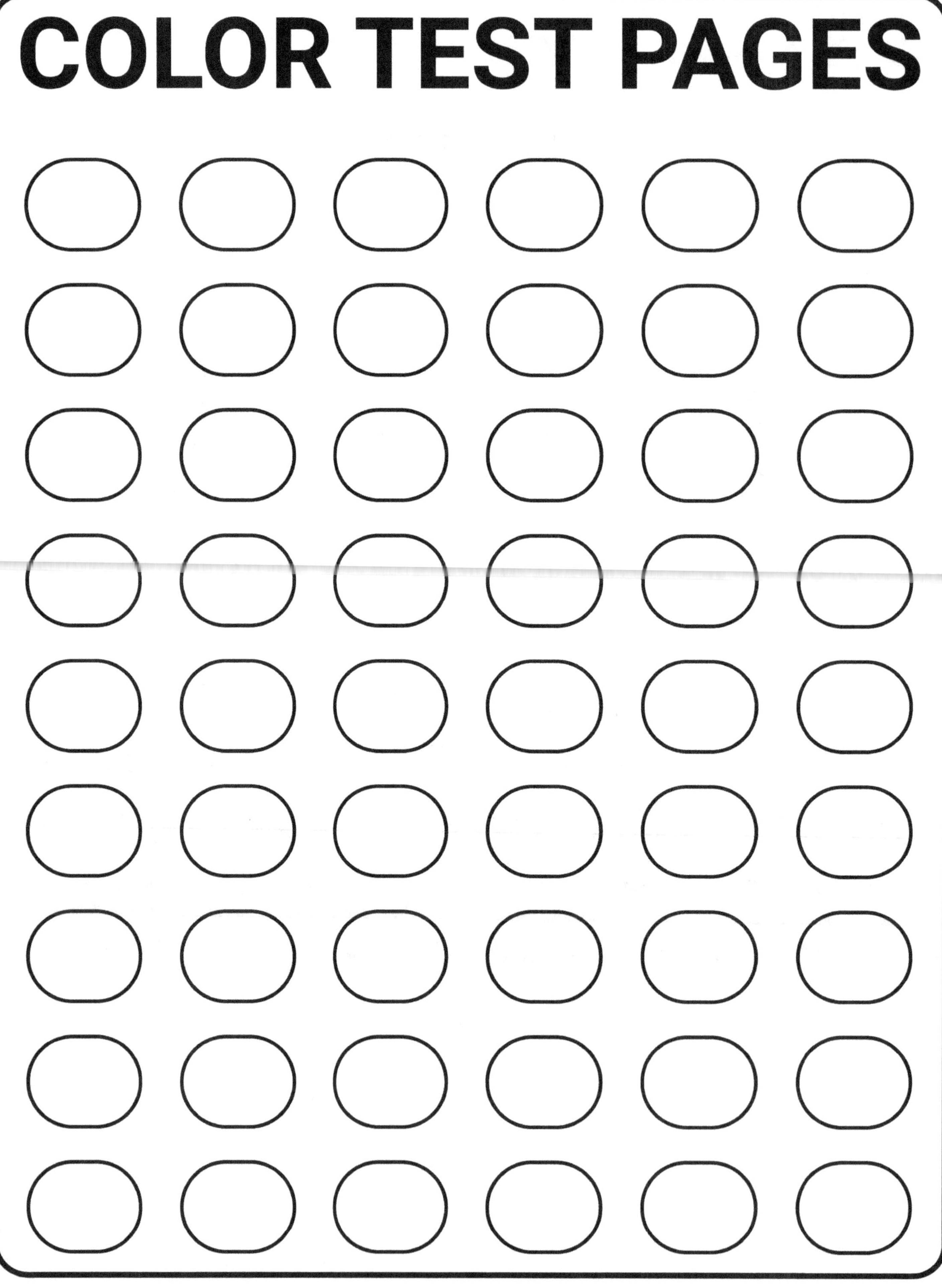

FUN FACTS ABOUT AXOLOTLS.

AXOLOTLS ARE AMPHIBIANS NATIVE TO MEXICO.

FUN FACTS ABOUT AXOLOTLS.

THEY HAVE FUNNY FEATHERY GILLS ON THEIR HEADS TO HELP THEM BREATHE.

FUN FACTS ABOUT AXOLOTLS.

AXOLOTLS CAN COME IN DIFFERENT COLORS LIKE BLACK, WHITE, GOLD, AND MORE!

THESE CUTE CREATURES LOVE TO EAT SMALL BUGS AND FISH.

AXOLOTLS ARE LIKE SUPERHEROES BECAUSE THEY CAN GROW BACK LOST BODY PARTS, LIKE THEIR TAILS!

FUN FACTS ABOUT AXOLOTLS.

THEY ARE GREAT AT SWIMMING AND CAN EVEN LIVE ON LAND TOO.

FUN FACTS ABOUT AXOLOTLS.

AXOLOTLS ARE VERY FRIENDLY AND LIKE TO MAKE FRIENDS WITH OTHER ANIMALS.

THEIR NAME SOUNDS FUNNY, BUT IT MEANS "WATER-DOG" IN AN OLD LANGUAGE.

FUN FACTS ABOUT AXOLOTLS.

THEY HAVE POOR EYESIGHT BUT RELY ON THEIR SENSES OF SMELL AND TOUCH TO LOCATE PREY.

FUN FACTS ABOUT AXOLOTLS.

EVEN THOUGH THEY LOOK LIKE FISH, AXOLOTLS ARE ACTUALLY SPECIAL AMPHIBIANS.

FUN FACTS ABOUT AXOLOTLS.

AXOLOTLS LOVE TO PLAY HIDE-AND-SEEK IN THE WATER!

AXOLOTLS HAVE BIG, CURIOUS EYES THAT HELP THEM EXPLORE THEIR UNDERWATER WORLD.

FUN FACTS ABOUT AXOLOTLS.

THEY WIGGLE THEIR BODIES TO MOVE AROUND AND HAVE FUN IN THE WATER.

FUN FACTS ABOUT AXOLOTLS.

AXOLOTLS ARE LIKE MAGIC BECAUSE THEY CAN LIVE FOR A LONG TIME, EVEN UP TO 15 YEARS!

FUN FACTS ABOUT AXOLOTLS.

THESE AMAZING ANIMALS ARE VERY GENTLE AND LOVE TO BE GENTLY PETTED BY THEIR HUMAN FRIENDS.

FUN FACTS ABOUT AXOLOTLS.

AXOLOTLS HAVE SUPER STRONG SENSES OF SMELL TO HELP THEM FIND YUMMY FOOD.

THEY LIKE TO SWIM TOGETHER WITH THEIR FRIENDS AND FAMILY IN BIG GROUPS.

FUN FACTS ABOUT AXOLOTLS.

EVEN THOUGH THEY LOOK A BIT SILLY, AXOLOTLS ARE VERY SMART AND CAN LEARN LOTS OF COOL TRICKS.

FUN FACTS ABOUT AXOLOTLS.

SOMETIMES THEY LIKE TO PLAY PEEK-A-BOO BY HIDING BEHIND ROCKS AND SURPRISING THEIR FRIENDS!

AXOLOTLS ARE SUPERSTARS IN THE UNDERWATER WORLD, AND THEY BRING LOTS OF JOY TO EVERYONE WHO MEETS THEM!

FUN FACTS ABOUT AXOLOTLS.

THEY WIGGLE THEIR TAILS TO SWIM GRACEFULLY THROUGH THE WATER, LIKE LITTLE MERMAIDS.

FUN FACTS ABOUT AXOLOTLS.

SOMETIMES THEY HAVE SILLY DREAMS WHILE THEY SLEEP UNDERWATER, JUST LIKE US!

FUN FACTS ABOUT AXOLOTLS.

AXOLOTLS ARE EXPERT HUNTERS AND CAN CATCH THEIR FOOD WITH LIGHTNING-FAST REFLEXES.

THEY HAVE UNIQUE PERSONALITIES AND CAN BE SHY OR OUTGOING, JUST LIKE PEOPLE.

AXOLOTLS HAVE CUTE LITTLE FRILLY GILLS THAT HELP THEM BREATHE UNDERWATER AND LOOK LIKE FAIRY WINGS.

AXOLOTLS ARE EXCELLENT JUMPERS AND CAN LEAP OUT OF THE WATER TO CATCH TASTY TREATS.

AXOLOTLS ARE MASTERS OF CAMOUFLAGE AND CAN BLEND INTO THEIR SURROUNDINGS TO STAY SAFE

THEY HAVE SUPER-SENSITIVE SKIN THAT CAN DETECT EVEN THE TINIEST VIBRATIONS IN THE WATER.

AXOLOTLS ARE NATURAL-BORN EXPLORERS AND LOVE TO INVESTIGATE EVERY NOOK AND CRANNY OF THEIR UNDERWATER WORLD.